Cocktails

Cocktails

An easy-to-follow illustrated guide to
making and serving delicious cocktails

AMANDA O'NEILL

p

About the Author

Amanda O'Neill lives in Leicestershire, England, with her family and a
pack of Chihuahuas. Educated at the Universities of Exeter and London,
she has written books on a range of subjects from mythology to the
decorative arts.

This is a Parragon Book
This edition published in 2001

Parragon
Queen Street House
4 Queen Street
Bath BA1 1HE, UK

Designed, packaged and produced by
Stonecastle Graphics Ltd

ISBN: 0-75256-334-3

Photography by Pinpoint
Edited by Philip de Ste. Croix

Manufactured in China

Contents

Understanding Cocktails

THERE IS just enough ritual to the mixing of a cocktail to establish a distinct air of celebration. This is not just a matter of pouring a drink, but of melding a variety of flavours into an harmonious whole. On the other hand, the mystique of mixing is not nearly as complicated as it appears, once you take into account a few basic principles.

The earliest definition of the cocktail calls it 'a stimulating liquor, composed of *spirits* of any kind, *sugar*, *water*, and *bitters*'. This remains the basic pattern: spirit, mixer (nowadays a rather more positive element than sugar and water) and flavouring. Many recipes may seem more complicated than this, but it should always be possible to break them down into the three basic elements.

The base spirit is the keynote of the cocktail that establishes its identity and provides the key taste. The mixer should highlight this taste, but never overpower it. The flavouring, the smallest ingredient in terms of quantity, adds that essential extra detail without which a cocktail is just two drinks sloshed together. The one vital rule of cocktail making is that all elements should enhance the base spirit, not drown it.

Some recipes call for more than one spirit or liqueur element. This can work well if these complement rather than counter each other. However, a few 'killer cocktails' pile spirit upon spirit with the sole aim of producing as lethal a load of alcohol as possible, regardless of taste. Such mixtures, with menacing names like Terminator or Zombie indicating their effect, miss the whole point of the cocktail, and are best left to those young enough to believe you aren't having fun if you can still stand up.

Of course, with more than 10,000 different cocktails recognized across the world today, the variations are endless. A much wider range of spirits, liqueurs and cordials is available to us than to previous generations; and additional ingredients such as cream, eggs or liquidized fruit have become part of the repertoire.

Cocktail recipes are not written in stone. Every barman has his own variations, and you will find different versions of nearly all the recipes in this book. Don't let this confuse you – just take it as an invitation to trust your taste buds and feel free to adapt any recipe to suit yourself.

Garnishes provide a finishing touch. Some, such as citrus peel, may form an integral part of a cocktail's flavour. Others, like paper parasols and even the ubiquitous cocktail cherry, are purely decorative. Not all cocktails require a garnish. As a general rule, a simple garnish like a lemon or orange slice sets off the colour of a clear cocktail, while

more elaborate decoration is best reserved for glamorous tropical cocktails. Traditional garnishes can look heavy on thick creamy or eggy mixtures, which are better suited by a light dusting of spices such as ground cinnamon or freshly grated nutmeg. Suggestions for appropriate garnishes are distributed among the recipes in this book, but don't be afraid to experiment.

Equipment
You do not actually need a full bartender's kit. The essentials are:
- a cocktail shaker for shaken drinks
- a mixing glass (or a plain glass jug) and a stirrer (a long-handled bar spoon is ideal) for stirred drinks
- an electric blender for blended drinks
- some form of cocktail measure

A fruit knife, vegetable peeler, chopping board and lemon squeezer are handy for preparing good-looking garnishes. Apart from that, all you really need are your taste buds – and a few friends to invite round to enjoy the party!

A Mixed History

SOME SAY the cocktail was invented in 1779 by New York barmaid Betsy Flanagan, when she served stolen chicken for dinner and defiantly used the cocks' tailfeathers to garnish the drinks. Others say it began in Bordeaux, France, as a popular drink called *le coquetel*. A tongue-in-cheek (and tongue-twister) tale involves Aztec princess Xochitl, whose name became corrupted to our 'cocktail', while a more prosaic suggestion derives the name from 'cocktail' (docked) horses, which (like the drink) are often of mixed breeding.

All that can be said for certain is that the cocktail was established as one of life's pleasures by 1806, when the word first appears in print. Throughout the 19th century the cocktail craze spread across America and on to Europe. Britain's first cocktail bar opened in 1851 – to be closed within months on the grounds that it was 'dangerous...for the morals of young persons'.

But the spread of the cocktail was unstoppable. The first book of cocktail recipes appeared in 1862. Today we still relish some 19th century classics – the Manhattan, Mint Julep and Sherry Cobbler among them – though perhaps not Queen Victoria's favourite tipple, an unlikely mix of her favourite Scotch whisky and claret.

As every parent knows, anything becomes more desirable when it is banned, and in the 1920s America's Prohibition laws barring the manufacture and sale of alcoholic drinks gave cocktails the ultimate boost. The 1920s were the quintessential Cocktail Age. Quite apart from enjoying the fashionable frisson of drinking in illegal speak-easies, drinkers found that illicitly made 'moonshine' and 'bathtub gin' needed mixers to disguise the unpleasant taste.

Across the Atlantic, cocktails were equally fashionable as the tipple of 'Bright Young Things'. The cocktail party was born, probably an American innovation which spread swiftly to Britain. It was a more convenient form of entertainment than the formal dinner party, and filled that dreary gap between tea and dinner.

Over subsequent decades, cocktails drifted in and out of fashion, but never entirely faded away. The 1970s saw another wave of cocktail creativity. Some of the new cocktails were deliberately outrageous, even silly – garishly coloured, overladen with alcohol, or saddled with over-the-top, drag-queen names. Others were more durable, including the various

creamy cocktails which appeared in this era. As a wider range of high-quality spirits became available, the 1990s saw a revival of cocktail classics as well as the introduction of a wave of new, post-modern cocktails using innovatory combinations of ingredients.

The image of cocktails has swung to and fro over the past two centuries. They have been seen as glamorous and suave, unsophisticated and even vulgar, respectably conventional, or downright shocking. Today's range of cocktails provides a range of images to suit all tastes. Mix yourself a drink – whether summer refresher or winter warmer – and settle down to enjoy it!

Whisky

WHISKY (Scotland) or whiskey (Ireland and the USA) takes its name from the Gaelic *uisge beatha*, 'water of life', and its history is intimately bound up with that of the Scottish and Irish Gaels. Irish legend credits St. Patrick with its creation back in the 5th century. History is vaguer, but it seems likely that Irish and Scots stills were up and running in the early medieval period.

Centuries later, Celtic emigrants took their skill with the still to North America. American whiskey was born, to play its part in the Wild West and to add a zest to the gangster era of Prohibition.

Whisk(e)y is made from a distillation of malted barley, unmalted barley, maize or rye. Scotland's famous malt whisky is produced from malted barley, heated over a peat fire to give the characteristic smoky aroma. A milder form of Scotch is grain whisky, generally made from maize; many brands of Scotch are blended malt and grain. Irish whiskey is made from malted but unsmoked barley, and is triple distilled. From the US come rye whiskey, made from at least 51 per cent rye, and bourbon, made with over 51 per cent corn (maize) and aged in charred oak barrels to give the characteristic flavour.

The strong flavour of whisk(e)y blends successfully with a fairly limited range of ingredients. For Scotch-based cocktails, a blended whisky is usually used. Where rye whiskey is called for, look for the true Kentucky rye; if this is unobtainable, the sweeter bourbon can be substituted.

Manhattan

The birthplace of what is probably the most famous of all whisky-based cocktails, the Manhattan Club, was founded in 1864 as a Democratic counter to the Republican Union League.

2 measures rye
1 measure sweet vermouth
1 dash Angostura bitters
5 or 6 ice cubes
Maraschino cherry for garnish

Place the ice cubes in a mixing glass, and pour the rye and vermouth over them and add a dash of bitters. Stir until well chilled and strain into a cocktail glass. Garnish with a cherry submerged in the drink. For a Dry Manhattan, omit the bitters and substitute dry vermouth for sweet.

BANNED BOURBON

Bourbon, which takes its name from Bourbon County, Kentucky, is Kentucky's leading export yet cannot be sold legally within that state. Nearly 70 years after Prohibition ended, most of Kentucky remains 'dry'.

NEW YORK CLASSIC

The Manhattan was invented at New York's Manhattan Club in the 1870s for Jennie Jerome (Lady Randolph Churchill, mother of Sir Winston). Sweet vermouth and bitters formed the basis of many cocktails of the period. Today bourbon often replaces rye.

Mint Julep

The favourite drink of the Deep
South, the Mint Julep has been the
traditional beverage of the Kentucky
Derby for nearly a century.

4 or 5 fresh mint leaves
1 teaspoon sugar
1 teaspoon water
1 measure bourbon
Crushed ice
Sprig of mint for garnish

Place the mint leaves, sugar and water in a julep
glass and crush them together until the sugar
dissolves. Add the bourbon, then top up the glass
with crushed ice. Garnish with a sprig
of fresh mint.

ORANGES AND LEMONS

A twist of orange or lemon peel makes an
attractive garnish for many cocktails. With a
very sharp knife, shave fine strips off the zest
of the fruit, taking care not to include any of
the white pith. Twist a strip over the surface
of the drink to release a fine spray of
essential oil from the peel into the glass, then
drop the twist into the cocktail.

Old-fashioned

As its name suggests, another old favourite.
Everyone has their own recipe; this one should
avoid an old-fashioned hangover.

1 teaspoon sugar
2 dashes Angostura bitters
A little water
Ice
Rye
Cherry and lemon twist/orange slice for
garnish

Place the sugar in a glass, add the bitters and
water and stir until the sugar
dissolves. Fill the glass with ice, top
up with rye and garnish.

Commodore

Perhaps this owes its naval title to the inclusion
of lime juice, once a staple of the Royal Navy's
on-board provisions to ward off scurvy.

4 measures rye
1 measure fresh lime juice
2 dashes orange bitters
Optional sugar to taste.

Shake all ingredients together in a shaker,
strain and serve

A BIT ABOUT BITTERS

Bitters are spirits infused with strongly
flavoured herbs, roots, bark or peel. Originally
developed for medicinal purposes, they came
into their own last century as a cocktail
ingredient. Angostura bitters, made in Trinidad,
originated as a malaria cure but has since
become an essential part of many classic
cocktails such as the Manhattan and Pink Gin.

Whiskey Sour

Sours can be made with any spirit, shaken with fresh citrus fruit juice and a sweetener and usually enhanced with a little egg white.

3 measures Scotch
2 measures freshly squeezed lemon juice
1 measure gomme syrup
Dash egg white
Lemon slice to garnish

Shake all ingredients in a shaker. Strain into the glass and garnish with a lemon slice.

SCOTTISH SECRET, AMERICAN ANSWER

Legend claims that the recipe for Drambuie – Scotch malt whisky blended with herbs and heather honey – was presented to the Mackinnon family of Skye by Bonnie Prince Charlie himself. Scotland now boasts a wide range of whisky-based liqueurs, to which America's answer is Southern Comfort, created in New Orleans in the 1860s – whiskey flavoured with peach and a further 100 ingredients!

GOMME SYRUP

Gomme syrup (also called simple or sugar syrup) is an element in many cocktails. Slowly bring to the boil equal quantities of water and white sugar. Simmer the mixture until the sugar has dissolved, producing a clear syrup. Allow this to cool, then pour it into a clean bottle. Refrigerated, it will keep for some months.

Los Angeles

The reason why this restorative potion is named for the City of Angels (or 'Smog City', if you prefer) remains obscure. Perhaps because the Earth quakes if too many are imbibed!

2 measures Scotch
1 measure lemon juice
1 egg
Dash sweet vermouth

Shake all ingredients together in a shaker. Strain into the serving glass.

Rusty Nail

Sir Kingsley Amis, a man who well knew his advocaat from his egg-nog, described this cocktail as 'delicious but dangerous'.

2 measures Scotch
1 measure Drambuie
Ice cubes (optional)
Twist of lemon peel

Pour the Scotch and Drambuie into a glass, with or without ice cubes according to taste. Drop in the lemon twist.

Shamrock

Whether or not St. Patrick was the inventor of
Irish whiskey, this drink is a favourite on his feast
day, 17 March.

1 measure Irish whiskey
1 measure dry vermouth
3 dashes green Chartreuse
3 dashes crème de menthe

Stir all ingredients together in a mixing glass
and then pour.

Royalist

Presumably this drink derives its name from its
bourbon base. Of the Bourbon line of French
kings, Louis XVI did not let it go to his head.

1 measure bourbon
2 measures dry vermouth
1 measure Bénédictine
Dash peach bitters

Stir all ingredients together in a mixing glass
and then serve.

SHAKEN, NOT STIRRED

When a cocktail is to be shaken, put all the ingredients with a generous amount of crushed ice into the shaker, hold on the stopper firmly, and shake rapidly up and down, until the outside of the shaker is frosted. Strain the mixture into a glass. (Any fizzy ingredients should be reserved and added afterwards.)

Maple Leaf

One might expect a drink named for the national emblem of Canada to feature Canadian Club whiskey, but it owes its title to the maple syrup used as an ingredient.

2 measures bourbon
1 measure lemon juice
1 teaspoon maple syrup
Crushed ice

Shake all ingredients together in a shaker. Strain into the serving glass.

THE MONKS' CLASSICS

The famous herb-flavoured liqueur Chartreuse has been produced by monks near Grenoble, France since the 17th century. The two strengths, green (55% vol) and yellow (43%), owe their rich colours to natural ingredients alone. The recipe is a closely-kept secret, known only to three monks who are only allowed to talk, to each other, once a week. Another French classic, Bénédictine, is said to have been invented by one of the monks of Fécamp Abbey in Normandy in 1510, and – despite a century's interruption after the French Revolution – it is still distilled there today.

Brandy

BRANDY IS distilled from fermented grape juice, without the addition of any other spirits. It is made worldwide, the quality depending on the soil where the grapes are grown as well as on maturing methods. The two greatest brandies, Cognac and Armagnac, both come from France.

Brandy takes its name from the German *brandtwein*, 'burnt (i.e. distilled) wine'. However, it originated in Spain, following the 8th century Moorish conquest of Andalucia. The Moors introduced distilling, an art they used to create cosmetics and perfumes. Eventually Spanish vintners in the city of Jerez began distilling a primitive brandy which they used to fortify their local wine – creating the product we know as sherry. The first brandy, then, was an ingredient in sherry. Not until the 19th century did the Spanish treat it as a product in its own right.

Meanwhile the French adopted and refined the art of making brandy. Of France's two premier brandy-producing regions, Armagnac was the leader, distilling spirits as early as 1411. Cognac did not enter the field until the 17th century, but then it gained the ascendancy as a result of better transport facilities.

Brandy is less versatile as a cocktail element than gin or vodka, but it can be very successful. Choose your brandy with care. Spanish brandy is dark and sweet, American brandy generally lighter and fruitier than European brands, and Armagnac is best avoided for cocktails, where it tends to be overpowering.

American Beauty

This sumptuous drink packs quite a punch, so beware: too many beauties may bring out the beast in you!

1 measure brandy
1 measure dry vermouth
1 measure grenadine
1 measure orange juice
1 dash white crème de menthe
2–3 dashes port

Shake together all the ingredients except the port. Strain, and pour the port gently on to the surface so that it floats on top. The glowing colours, a rich tawny-orange set off by a ruby crown of port, are garnish enough.

BRANDY FOR THE PARSON

Five and twenty ponies trotting through the dark – Brandy for the Parson, 'Baccy for the clerk.' Kipling romanticized the smuggling 'Gentlemen' of his poem; the reality was different. It was estimated in 1777 that more than 2,000,000 gallons of brandy (and even more gin and rum) were smuggled annually from France to England. A powerful 'mafia' controlled the trade, and customs officers who would not be bribed were frequently murdered.

FRUIT BRANDIES

While true brandy is always made from grapes, other fruit brandies abound. The queen of them all is Calvados, an apple brandy from Normandy in France. Others use fruits ranging from plums to holly berries. Austria's versions are known as schnapps and include the world's rarest spirit, Elsbeer, made from the fruit of the wild service tree.

Sidecar

Mixing the perfect Sidecar takes practice, to achieve the right balance between the tart lemon and sweet Cointreau flavours.

2 measures cognac
1 measure Cointreau
1 measure lemon juice
Lemon twist to garnish

Shake the ingredients and strain the mixture over ice into a chilled cocktail glass with a sugar-frosted rim. Garnish with a long coiling lemon twist anchored at the base of the glass with ice cubes.

Brandy Alexander

In the 1970s, this was the 'in' drink of disco land. Today, it has found another niche as the ideal after-dinner glass, served with the coffee.

1 measure brandy
1 measure brown crème de cacao
1 measure double cream
Crushed ice
freshly grated nutmeg

Shake brandy, crème de cacao and cream together with crushed ice. Strain the creamy mixture into a cocktail glass, and dust nutmeg over the surface. For an attractive variation, serve with a cinnamon stick.

MYSTERIOUS MOTORCYCLIST

The origins of the Sidecar are obscure, but it was probably invented in Paris during the First World War. Legend says that its creator always arrived in his favourite bar in a motorcycle sidecar. Paris traffic being what it is, he probably needed to unwind with this sweet and sour classic after his ride!

Horse's Neck

This refreshing drink can also be made with gin or with bourbon, adding a couple of dashes of Angostura bitters. The same name is also used for a brandy and champagne pick-me-up.

I measure brandy
Dry ginger ale
A lemon or lime spiral
Ice cubes

Drop the lemon spiral into a tall glass, and anchor it with ice cubes. Pour in the brandy, and top up with ginger ale. In barman-speak, this isn't a cocktail but a highball (a long drink comprising a spirit, ice and dry ginger or soda water) – probably the best known of its clan.

ALEXANDER THE GREAT?

No one is quite sure to whom the Brandy Alexander owes its name. Some cocktail historians point out that it became popular around 1911, when *Alexander's Ragtime Band* by Irving Berlin was an international hit. Others consider it an extension of 'Café Borgia' (coffee with chocolate or cacao flavouring), which itself was named after Pope Alexander VI – father of the famous Lucrezia and Cesare Borgia.

Golden Medallion

Orange juice and Galliano bring out the rich fruitiness of the brandy.

1 measure brandy
1 measure Galliano
1 measure fresh orange juice
Dash egg white
Grated orange zest

Shake the ingredients together, strain and serve. A little finely grated zest of orange peel sprinkled on top will set off the glowing colour. For an alternative garnish, pare a strip of rind from the orange (taking care to remove any white pith), fold the strip into a concertina and spear it on a cocktail stick.

THE ORANGE RANGE

Liqueurs come with many fruity flavours, but dried orange peel was probably the first to achieve favour (in the 17th century, when the Dutch invented Curaçao) and remains the most widely used. Most orange liqueurs, including Curaçao and Cointreau, use bitter oranges. Van der Hum is a South African version combining oranges and tangerines, macerated with spices in brandy.

SOUTH AMERICAN SPECIAL

Pisco, a South American brandy, was created by Spanish settlers in the 17th century. It takes its name from the town of Pisco in Peru, which itself was named after the local clay pots in which the brandy was stored. Today it is largely a speciality of Chile, although also produced in Peru and Bolivia.

First Night

A rich and warming concoction, ideal to calm the nerves before a first night – or to celebrate afterwards.

2 measures brandy
1 measure Van der Hum
1 measure Tia Maria
1 teaspoon cream

Shake all the ingredients together, strain and serve. An optional garnish is a light sprinkling of grated chocolate.

Pisco Sour

This is the national drink of Chile and Peru – a cooling drink ideal for the heat of South American summers, but deceptively strong.

2 measures Pisco
1 measure lemon juice
1 teaspoon caster sugar
Dash orange bitters (optional)
Egg white (optional)

Shake well and strain into glasses. The egg white is optional, but it does help to bind the flavours together – and also improves the drink's appearance. Gran Pisco, the driest (and strongest) version, is recommended.

Rum

IT'S A rum thing, but no one seems to know the origin of the name 'rum'. The drink itself, distilled from fermented sugar-cane juice or from molasses, originated in the 16th century as a by-product of the sugar industry in the Caribbean islands. In its early years, under the name of 'Kill-Devil' or 'Rumbullion', it was considered 'a hot hellish and terrible liquor' fit only to stupefy the slaves who worked the sugar plantations. Only later was it rendered into a drink considered fit for their masters.

Rum acquired its reputation as the favoured drink of both pirates (with a 'Yo ho ho and a bottle of rum!') and the lower decks of the Royal Navy for the practical reason that, unlike beer and wine, it remained drinkable on long cruises. By the 18th century it had became fashionable on land, in both England and the US. Rum houses served it as 'Rumfustian' with spices, or mixed with other spirits, wine or beer. Today it remains a classic mixer, blending particularly well with fruit juices and liqueurs in a variety of popular cocktails. The lighter white and golden rums create an effect quite different from the heavier, sweeter dark rums.

Piña Colada

One of the most popular of tropical cocktails, this is best made with fresh coconut milk, but coconut cream can be substituted.

*3 measures white or
golden rum
4 measures pineapple juice
2 measures coconut milk
2 scoops crushed ice
Slice of fresh pineapple to garnish*

Blend all ingredients together in a liquidizer. Serve in a tumbler – or, for a totally tropical effect, in a coconut shell. Garnish generously with pineapple and paper parasols, and with two straws.

RUM AND THE NAVY

In 1687, the Royal Navy allotted all ratings a daily ration of half a pint of rum plus occasional bonuses. 'What shall we do with the drunken sailor?' was a regular problem, but it was not until 1740 that Admiral Vernon, nicknamed 'Old Grog' from his grogram cloak, had the rum ration diluted with water a mix thereafter known as 'grog'. The grog ration, though reduced, was not discontinued until 1970.

Daiquiri

Invented by American mining engineers in Cuba's
Daiquiri mountains, the Daiquiri was perfected
(and enjoyed regularly by writer Ernest
Hemingway) in the El Floridita bar in Havana.

3 measures white rum
1 measure fresh lime juice
3 dashes gomme syrup
Ice cubes

Shake the rum, lime juice and syrup together and
strain over ice into a cocktail glass. Simplicity is
the keynote of the perfect Daiquiri, so it calls for
no garnish.

Banana Daiquiri

Fans of fantasy writer Terry Pratchett will know
this as the 'Bananana dakry', a favourite tipple of
the witch Nanny Ogg even if she can't spell it.

3 measures white rum
1 measure crème de banane
Juice of half a lime
Half a banana
2 scoops of crushed ice

Blend in a liquidizer, but not for too long or the
drink will become too diluted. Pile it into a large
goblet and serve with fat straws. Garnish with a
slice of banana, cut diagonally and perched on
the rim of the glass.

VARIATIONS ON A THEME

For a classic Frozen Daiquiri, mix the rum, lime juice and syrup in a blender with crushed ice, then strain it to avoid over-dilution. For a Mint Daiquiri, a Cuban favourite, add Cointreau and a handful of mint leaves. Alternatively, add fresh fruit, replace the syrup with the related fruit liqueur, and blend together for fruity Daiquiris like Coconut, Peach or Strawberry.

Apricot Lady

A rich golden colour redolent of tropical sunrises matches the mellow flavour.

2 measures golden rum
2 measures apricot brandy
1 measure fresh lime juice
3 dashes orange curaçao
2 dashes egg white
Small scoop crushed ice
Orange slice for garnish

Blend all ingredients in a liquidizer; strain, and serve with short straws. Garnish with a slice of orange or, if you prefer, apricot wedges.

DRESSING UP

An exotic garnish enhances many tropical cocktails, as long as it does not resemble a fruit salad stuck in at random. Try reflecting the ingredients with matching fruit wedges or slices, complementing the colour by floating borage flowers or nasturtium petals on top, or giving ice cubes a starring role by dropping grated lemon rind, mint leaves, olives, etc. into the ice tray before freezing the ice cubes.

Palm Breeze

As refreshing as its name, this cocktail
nevertheless packs quite a punch – too many and
you might be blown out to sea!

3 measures dark rum
2 measures yellow Chartreuse
1 part crème de cacao
Juice of half a lime
Dash grenadine

Mix all ingredients in a cocktail shaker, strain and
pour into a glass. A long twist of lime peel makes
a stylish garnish.

Cuba Libre

This long cooler is yet another of the old
favourites invented in Cuba around the turn of
the century, when the Spanish-American War
freed Cuba from Spanish domination – hence the
name, 'free Cuba'.

1 measure white rum
Juice of half a lime
Cola
Lime slice for garnish

Half fill a highball glass with ice, add the rum and
lime juice, top up with cola, and stir. Garnish with
a slice of lime, or drop the half-lime shell into the
glass, and serve with straws.

Shanghai

Dark rum, with its stronger, sweeter taste, perfectly complements the dryness of the anise-flavoured pastis.

4 measures dark rum
1 measure pastis
3 measures lemon juice
2 dashes grenadine
Lemon slice and cherry for garnish

Shake all ingredients together and strain into a glass. Garnish with a lemon slice and cherry speared on a cocktail stick.

PASS THE PASTIS

Anise-based spirits such as pastis have long been popular in Mediterranean countries. Pastis is made by macerating herbal ingredients, notably aniseed and liquorice, in spirit to create a delicate and refreshing yellow aperitif. It is not a common cocktail constituent, but one well worth trying.

A DASH OF FLAVOUR

Grenadine, a pomegranate-flavoured, red-coloured, non-alcoholic cordial, is used in many cocktail recipes. Use a brand made with natural ingredients, and apply with a light hand, or the sweet flavour may overpower the other ingredients.

Casablanca

Redolent with tropical colour and flavour, this
dream of a drink was named for the classic 1942
film starring Humphrey Bogart. Serve it
again, Sam!

3 measures white rum
4 measures pineapple juice
2 measures coconut cream
2 dashes grenadine
2 scoops crushed ice
Pineapple and cherry to garnish

Blend all ingredients together and serve with two
straws. Garnish with a pineapple wedge topped by
a maraschino cherry.

Jamaica Joe

Rich and pungent Jamaica rum will not be
overpowered by the sweetness of the Tia Maria
and advocaat (an egg-and-brandy liqueur).

I measure Jamaica rum
I measure Tia Maria
I measure advocaat
Dash grenadine
Nutmeg to garnish

Shake the rum, Tia Maria and advocaat together
before adding the grenadine. Pour into a glass,
and dust lightly with freshly grated nutmeg.

CHERRY RIPE

The maraschino cherry has become so much part of the cocktail tradition that we habitually speak of 'cocktail cherries'. It may be dropped straight into the glass, or speared on a cocktail stick, alone or accompanied by a slice of fruit. Unlike most fruit garnishes, the cherry rarely influences the taste of the drink and is included mainly for visual effect.

Blue Hawaiian

An eye-catching drink, colourfully garnished, which is bound to banish the blues and transport you to warmer climes.

2 measures white rum
1 measure blue curaçao
1 measure coconut cream
2 measures pineapple juice
Crushed ice
fruit for garnish

Mix the curaçao, coconut cream and rum in an electric blender until the colour is even throughout. Add the pineapple juice, and blend again into a thick froth before pouring over crushed ice. Garnish lavishly with an assortment of fruit wedges (pineapple, pear, lime, etc.) crammed on to a cocktail stick, and serve with two straws.

AUNT MARY

Coffee beans, vanilla and other spices, and a touch of chocolate, are infused in Jamaican cane spirit to make the coffee liqueur Tia Maria. Its unusual name ('Aunt Mary') is ascribed to a 17th century adventure. When a Jamaican estate was attacked by raiders, the maidservant Maria rescued her young mistress and the family's treasured liqueur recipe, which was later renamed in her honour.

Gin

JUNIPER BERRIES give gin both its characteristic flavour and its name (from Dutch *genever*, 'juniper'). Like many spirits, it first saw light as a medicine, achieving widespread use in the 14th century as a supposed prophylactic against the Black Death. Only later did it become popular as an alcoholic drink, first in Holland and Belgium.

In 1689, Dutch prince William of Orange mounted the English throne, bringing 'Hollands gin' with him. It was not an unmixed blessing. By the early 18th century, cheap and plentiful gin had become a major social problem in England. The poor could become 'drunk for a penny, dead drunk for tuppence' and did so with enthusiasm, as is depicted in the horrors of the engraving 'Gin Lane' by William Hogarth. By 1750, the English were drinking gin at the rate of an astonishing 20 million gallons a year.

By the end of the 19th century, changing social conditions had encouraged the disreputable drink of the poor to move upmarket, becoming particularly fashionable in 1920s London and (despite the poor reputation of 'bathtub gin') in Prohibition America.

Gin was at the heart of the rise of cocktails, and remains the classic cocktail base. There are two broad types: British (London/dry) and Dutch (Hollands/Geneva schnapps). In the latter, the grain alcohol is less highly purified and retains more grain flavour. Some recipes specify which type to use: if in doubt, go for a London gin.

Dry Martini

The most famous of all cocktails, the Dry Martini
is also one of the most varied, the ratio of gin to
dry vermouth (which started out as 50:50) now
ranging from 3:1 to 25:1 according to taste. (The
great W.C. Fields claimed that merely allowing
light to reflect through the vermouth bottle on to
the gin was sufficient.)

3 measures gin
1 measure dry vermouth
Ice
Green olive for garnish
Lemon zest

Stir the gin and vermouth in a mixing
glass with plenty of ice, and strain into
a chilled cocktail glass. Squeeze the zest
of lemon peel over the top, or drop
in a lemon twist, and garnish
with a green olive.

SHAKEN OR STIRRED?

Since the Dry Martini was invented in 1911 in
the bar of New York's Knickerbocker Hotel,
aficionados have argued whether it should be
shaken or stirred. Like the proportion of
vermouth, it's a matter of personal preference.
Popular variations include the Vodka Martini
beloved of James Bond, who memorably insisted
on the use of a shaker.

Singapore Sling

Created in 1915 at the Raffles Hotel, Singapore, this is a refreshing classic which has never gone out of favour.

2 measures gin
1 measure cherry brandy
1 measure lemon juice
Soda water
Sprig of mint and orange slice for garnish

Shake the first three ingredients together and strain into a tall glass. Top up with soda, and garnish. The fresh mint adds an aromatic savour to this delicious cooler.

Gimlet

The Gimlet has been around since at least 1928, when it is first recorded in print. Lovers of crime novels will know it as the drink of Raymond Chandler's hard-boiled detective Philip Marlowe.

2 measures gin
1 measure lime juice cordial
Ice cubes
Optional soda water

Stir the gin and cordial together, and pour over ice cubes. The amount of lime used depends on personal taste: it should complement, not mask the gin. Fresh lime juice makes the drink cloudy, but some prefer its flavour. Top up with soda water if you're in the mood for a long drink.

Mediterranean

Whatever the weather, this eye-catching drink should transport your imagination to the blue skies and seas of the Mediterranean.

2 measures gin
1 measure blue curaçao
Lemonade
Ice cubes

Put ice cubes in a glass and pour the gin and curaçao over them. Top up with lemonade. The exotic colour needs no garnish to set it off.

SLINGS

The Gin Sling, a long drink of gin and lemon, whose name comes from the German *schlingen*, 'to swallow', is one of the oldest basic cocktails, dating back to before 1800. Variations on the theme include not only the Singapore Sling but the Raffles Bar Sling (substitute ginger beer for the soda water) and Straits Sling (add a dash of Bénédictine).

White Lady

The delicious White Lady was invented in Paris in 1919, at the famous Harry's Bar, and remains a popular favourite.

2 measures London Dry gin
1 measure Cointreau
1 measure lemon juice
Dash egg white
Crushed ice
Cherry for garnish

Shake the ingredients thoroughly until the outside surface of the shaker is freezing cold, then strain the drink into a cocktail glass. A maraschino cherry adds the finishing touch to this delicately tinted mix with its snow-white, frothy topping.

Pink Gin

Long associated with British naval officers' wardrooms and with elderly colonels chatting in their clubs, this old-fashioned favourite is well worth reviving for its subtly aromatic flavour.

1 measure Plymouth gin
Angostura bitters
Iced water

Shake half a dozen drops of bitters into a spirit glass and twist the glass around to coat the inside. Tip out any excess before adding the gin, and top up with iced water. This can be made into a long drink by adding soda.

SOME OTHER LADIES

If you enjoy a White Lady, try some of its relations. For a Pink Lady, omit the lemon juice and substitute a measure of grenadine for the Cointreau. The exotic Blue Lady substitutes blue curaçao (and changes the ratio: use one measure of gin to two of curaçao), setting off the white foam topping to dramatic effect.

THE COLLINS CLAN

A bartender called Collins acquired some sort of immortality when he mixed gin with lemon, sugar and soda water to create the drink that bears his name, but nobody knows when or where, or even agrees on his first name. His mixture works well with other spirits, and a whole family of Collinses has evolved, including the Colonel Collins (bourbon), Jack Collins (apple brandy), Joe Collins (vodka) and Pierre Collins (cognac).

THE COLLINS GLASS

The tall Collins glass, intended for the cocktails bearing that name, has a large capacity which makes it ideal for any long drink.

John or Tom Collins

A 'sweet and sour' tang overlying an aromatic gin base makes this a great thirst-quencher, whichever name you give it.

1 measure London dry gin
Juice of 1 lemon
1 teaspoon gomme syrup
Soda water
Lemon slice for garnish

Half-fill a Collins glass with ice. Add the gin, lemon juice and gomme syrup, top up with soda water, and stir. Garnish with a slice of lemon, and serve with straws.

fallen Angel

The fragrances of mint and juniper might well tempt an angel to fall to with relish. Mint is a popular folk remedy to ease tension: in this combination, it should do the trick!

3 measures gin
I measure fresh lemon juice
2 dashes crème de menthe
Dash Angostura bitters
Crushed ice
Mint sprig for garnish

A simple one – just shake all the ingredients together and enjoy! To make the most of the mint flavour, rub mint leaves round the inside of the glass before pouring in the drink.

Inca

The legendary lost gold of the Incas – the 'sweat of the sun' to those sun-worshippers – inspired the name of this golden cocktail.

I measure gin
I measure sweet vermouth
I measure dry sherry
Dash orgeat syrup (a non-alcoholic almond-flavoured syrup)
Dash orange bitters

Pour all the ingredients into a glass and stir. This is one to serve ungarnished, to avoid distracting the tastebuds from the intriguing blend of flavours.

CRÈME DE MENTHE

Available in white or green versions, crème de menthe is made by infusing mint leaves with water to release the highly fragrant essential oils, which are then combined with neutral spirit. It is at its best used as a mixer rather than when drunk on its own.

Strawberry Dawn

A summer special, this fluffy concoction looks like an innocent milkshake, but is fragrant with gin.

1 measure gin
1 measure coconut cream
4 fresh strawberries
2 scoops crushed ice

Reserve one strawberry, complete with its hull, for garnish. Blend the other ingredients together – but not for too long, or you will end up with a watery mixture. Cut a slit in the side of the reserved strawberry and secure it on to the rim of the glass, hull outwards. Pour in the mixture and serve with short fat straws.

FRUIT GIN

Fruit-flavoured gin is easily made at home and adds extra richness and colour to cocktails. Take a litre of gin, 1lb/450g of soft fruit (strawberries, peaches, etc.) and 8oz/225g of caster sugar, place in a large, wide-necked jar and seal it tightly. Leave in a cool, dark place for a month, shaking gently once a week before straining the mixture through muslin and pouring it into a clean bottle for storage.

Vodka

THERE ARE two things everybody knows about vodka: it's Russian, and it has no taste. Neither is strictly true. Although the name is Russian (meaning 'little water'), this spirit was probably a Polish creation, which spread only later to Russia and the Baltic States. And, while some vodkas – those designed later for Western palates – taste of little, others are distinctively flavoured.

Like many other spirits, vodka began as a medicine; even after it was accepted as a social drink, it doubled up as a body rub and aftershave. By the 16th century vodka drinking was part of life in Poland and Russia. Whatever starch crops were available (today usually grain, potatoes or molasses) were used to produce as light and pure a spirit as possible, repeatedly distilled to remove the flavouring compounds which give whisky, rum and brandy their character. It was then often enlivened with herbs or spices.

In the West, vodka had a poor image until the 1940s, when clever marketing recreated it as the drink for sophisticates and it found a niche as a versatile mixer in cocktails. This led to the development of Western style vodkas, smooth and pure with a neutral smell and taste. Russian and Polish vodkas remain heavier, more flavoursome and more oily. Flavoured vodkas (lemon, pepper, rowan, etc.) have also become popular again.

Vodka is used in many classic cocktails and can be substituted for gin in any gin-based recipes. Western vodkas are most commonly used, but it is worth experimenting with other varieties to suit your own tastes.

Bloody Mary

Everyone has their own pet recipe for this, so don't be afraid to experiment. It's a classic hangover cure (sometimes prepared without vodka as a 'Virgin Mary') as well as a popular cocktail.

1 measure vodka
4 measures tomato juice
2 dashes Worcestershire sauce
White pepper
Celery salt
Dash lemon juice
Tabasco sauce to taste
Celery stick to garnish

Mix all the ingredients in a shaker and strain them into a highball glass. Garnish it with a celery stick, which may be used as a stirrer. As a variant, try using a pepper-flavoured vodka such as Pieprzowka or Absolut Peppar.

A GRASSY GLASS

A classic among flavoured vodkas is Zubrowka, a Polish regional speciality since the 17th century. It comes from the Bialowieska forest, last home of the rare European bison – whose favourite grazing, bison grass, provides its delicate vanilla flavour. Legend says that only grass on which the bison have urinated is used but perhaps most people would prefer not to know that!

WHAT'S IN A NAME?

The Bloody Mary failed to catch on when it was first invented, in Harry's New York Bar, Paris, in the 1920s. Possibly its original name, the 'Bucket of Blood', put people off! In America, rechristened 'The Red Snapper', it fared no better until some genius renamed it after Queen Mary Tudor (1553–58), known to history as 'Bloody Mary' for her persecution of Protestants.

Moscow Mule

The first part of the name is a misnomer for a
New York invention; but be warned by the second
part – this mule can pack a real kick!

2 measures Western vodka
3 measures ginger beer
Squeeze of lime juice
Ice cubes
Lime wedge and sprig of mint to garnish

Pour the vodka over the ice cubes, add the other
ingredients and stir. Serve in a tall glass, garnished
with a sprig of mint and a wedge of lime. Some
prefer to use lemon rather than lime juice; others
like to add a dash of Angostura bitters.

ENGINEERED IN THE EAST
The Harvey Wallbanger is a variant on the
well-known Screwdriver, a mix of vodka and
orange juice said to have been invented by
American engineers in the Middle East. The
name? Well, their equipment didn't include
swizzle sticks, so guess what they used to
stir their drinks!

A MULE WITH A KICK
The Moscow Mule was the drink that made
vodka take off in the USA. Invented to shift a
1940s Smirnoff surplus, it quickly multiplied
vodka sales sixfold. But a decade later anti-
Russian feeling set patriotic New York
bartenders marching to the slogan, 'We can do
without the Moscow Mule'. Smirnoff producers
hastily pointed out that their vodka was not
Russian, but an all-American product made
in Connecticut.

Harvey Wallbanger

Tradition says the Harvey who hit the wall after imbibing this concoction was a California surfer. Sounds like a real wipeout!

3 measures vodka
8 measures orange juice
2 teaspoons Galliano
Ice cubes
Orange slice for garnish

Half fill a highball glass with ice, pour vodka and orange over the ice cubes, and float Galliano on top; garnish with orange; serve with two straws. For a warming variant, try mixing a splash of ginger wine with the vodka and orange.

Salty Dog

Sharp and stimulating, this is one which may well call for 'a hair of the dog' next morning!

1 measure vodka
2 measures grapefruit juice
Ice cubes
Salt
Lemon wedge for garnish

Pour ingredients – first the vodka, then the grapefruit juice – over ice cubes in a salt-frosted glass. Garnish with a lemon wedge or lemon twist.

Rompope

This is Mexico's version of the better-known Dutch advocaat, a thick, yellow, custardy treat for the sweet-toothed.

4oz/400g can sweetened condensed milk
Half-pint/300ml chilled milk
4 egg yolks
Quarter teaspoon vanilla essence
Quarter pint/150ml vodka
Quarter teaspoon powdered cinnamon

Reserve the cinnamon, and blend all the other ingredients in a liquidizer at top speed for 45 seconds. Strain and cool. Pour into glasses, and dust with powdered cinnamon. For a finishing touch, add a cinnamon stick for a stirrer.

WITCHES' BREW

Strega, an Italian herbal liqueur, was invented in 1860. The flavour is created from a blend of 70 different botanical elements, among which mint and fennel predominate. It takes its name ('witch' in Italian) from legends of local witches who concocted secret (and probably more sinister) brews.

BLACK BEAUTY

The Vodka Martini, a variation on the classic gin-based Dry Martini, was made famous by James Bond. For a very different version, try it with one of the black vodkas which have recently appeared on the market. The dramatic colour and subtly different flavour are worth experiencing.

Black Russian

Complement the dark good looks of this cocktail with a side plate of dark delicacies such as black olives or caviar canapes.

2 measures Russian vodka
1 measure coffee liqueur
2 or 3 ice cubes

Pour the vodka and liqueur over the ice cubes in a tumbler or highball glass. A Russian vodka is recommended, but the coffee liqueur will be the predominant taste, so be sure to use a good brand such as Tia Maria or Kahlua. For a variant, try a Red Russian, using cranberry vodka instead of clear spirit.

Golden Tang

Summery colours combine with the autumnal flavours of fruit and herbs to produce a delicious and refreshing mix.

4 measures clear vodka
2 measures Strega
1 measure crème de banane
1 measure orange squash
Cherry and orange slices for garnish

Shake all ingredients together, strain into glass and garnish with a maraschino cherry.

Tequila

THE MEXICAN spirit tequila is a descendant of pulque, the staple alcoholic drink of the Aztec Empire. The Aztecs took their pulque, brewed from agave plants, very seriously. Over-indulgence in it was illegal and could even lead to the death penalty – except in the case of elderly labourers. They could drink as much as they liked from the age of 60, on the grounds that they were no longer of much use anyway.

When the Spanish conquistadors introduced distillation to Mexico, a stronger brew called mezcal was created, which is still made throughout the country. Later a superior version was created using only the blue agave, and took its name from the town of Tequila, where the distillation industry took off in the mid-18th century. Today tequila is produced only in two designated regions of Mexico: Tequila and Tepatitlán.

Tequila was first imported to the US in the 1870s. In 1916, American soldiers countering Zapata's raids during the Mexican Revolution adopted it.

Prohibition gave it a further boost – since it was distilled legally in Mexico, it only had to be smuggled over the border. After the Second World War writers like Jack Kerouac and William Burroughs made exotic Mexico fashionable, and tequila began to spread, achieving cult status from the false rumour that it contained the psychedelic drug mescaline.

Tequila has a distinctive oily taste. It comes in four varieties, white, gold, anejo and silver, depending on the ageing process. They are aged for different amounts of time. White tequila is the standard version; gold has been aged in white oak casks for up to four years, and anejo for at least one year. Silver tequila is aged in wax-lined casks for a mellower flavour.

Margarita

Invented in the 1950s, this was the drink that set tequila on the road to popularity. Legend says it owes its name to Margarita Sames, a 1940s socialite, but it is also credited to other ladies.

2 measures tequila
2 measures fresh lime juice
1 measure Cointreau
Crushed ice

Shake the ingredients together. Serve in a salt-frosted glass, using a cut section of lime to moisten the glass rim. Garnish with a lime wedge to squeeze into the drink. For a dramatically coloured variant, try replacing the Cointreau with blue curaçao.

THE BOTTLED WORM

Some brands of mezcal still pop a 'worm' into the bottle – actually a moth larva which feeds on the agave plant. Legend has it that eating the 'worm' passes on some of the spirit of the agave, while modern folklore claims (confusing mezcal with the unrelated drug mescaline) that it has an hallucinatory effect. However, the mezcal worm is unlikely to catch on as a cocktail garnish.

Tequila Sunrise

This 1965 creation enjoyed a considerable vogue in the 1970s, when it was the 'in' drink at ski resorts and singles bars, and inspired the title of a memorable hit song by the US band The Eagles.

I measure tequila
4 measures orange juice
2 dashes grenadine
Ice cubes
Slice of lime to garnish

Put ice cubes into a large highball glass, then squeeze the lime over the ice and drop it into the glass. Add the tequila and orange juice, then pour the grenadine in slowly so that it sinks to the bottom. It will infuse upwards gradually to create a colourful 'sunrise' effect. Serve with straws and stirrer or swizzle stick, and a speared cherry if desired.

DECORATIVE LIME SLICES

With a very sharp knife, cut fine longitudinal strips of rind from the surface of the fruit before cutting the lime into slices. Each slice will then bear an ornamental pattern of bands cut into the rind. Halve or quarter the slices before dropping them into a glass.

BLENDING

Cocktails which incorporate thick ingredients such as fruit purée or coconut milk are often mixed by blending in a liquidizer. Crushed ice is usually used in the blender rather than ice cubes, to avoid blunting its blades. To crush ice, place ice cubes within a folded cloth and smash them with a wooden mallet or the end of a rolling pin until the required fineness is required.

Silk Stockings

Smooth and luxurious, this makes a good pre-dinner drink – or a light substitute for dessert. Don't get legless!

3 measures tequila
2 measures white crème de cacao
3 measures fresh cream
Dash grenadine
1 scoop crushed ice
Cinnamon powder and cherry for garnish

Mix everything except the cinnamon and cherry in a blender. Pour it smoothly into a glass and dust the surface with cinnamon powder. Garnish with a cherry speared on a cocktail stick.

Mockingbird

A refreshing drink for a summer party. The delicate flavour of the tequila is perfectly complemented by the tartness of the grapefruit.

1 measure tequila
2 measures grapefruit juice
Dash lime juice
Ice cubes
Cherry garnish

Pour the ingredients over the ice cubes. Decorate with a maraschino cherry and serve with a stirrer.

Sourteq

This tequila variation on the classic Whiskey Sour (see p.14) has all the lemony sharpness of the original and makes an equally great thirst-quencher.

2 measures tequila
1 measure fresh lemon juice
2 dashes gomme syrup
Dash egg white
Lemon slice and cherry for garnish

Shake all ingredients thoroughly. Strain, garnish with cherry and lemon slice, and serve with a stirrer. For a Sourteq with a difference, try adding a splash of port to the mixture after it is shaken.

Sunrise

This fruity beauty is given a smooth, rich quality by the addition of cream, a cocktail fashion popularized in the 1970s.

2 measures tequila
1 measure Galliano
1 measure crème de banane
1 measure cream
1 dash grenadine
1 dash lemon juice
Crushed ice

Shake all ingredients together and strain into the glass. For the sweet-toothed, an unusual garnish can be made by grating a little dark chocolate over the top.

ALPINE SWEETNESS

The famous Italian herbal liqueur Galliano was
named for Major Giuseppe Galliano, hero of the
Italian-Abyssinian War (1895-96). Flavoured with
more than 40 Alpine plants as well as star
anise, vanilla and fennel, it is too sweet for
most tastes on its own but makes an ideal
cocktail ingredient.

Tequador

This is a version of the better-known Matador
without its relation's measure of Cointreau, an
omission which allows the flavour of the tequila
to come through more strongly.

3 measures tequila
4 measures pineapple juice
Dash lime juice
Crushed ice
Splash of grenadine
Crushed ice

Shake the first three ingredients together and
pour the mix over crushed ice. Splash with
grenadine and serve with straws. A sugar-frosted
glass suits this cocktail, which can also be
garnished with a pineapple chunk.

DRINK AND DRAGONS

The agave which forms the basis of tequila is
a large succulent, sometimes mistakenly called
a cactus but actually more nearly related to
the amaryllis. It takes its name from Greek
myth: Agave was the daughter of the hero
Cadmus, who sowed dragon's teeth from which
sprang up armed warriors. Those who drink
too much of her namesake may also find
themselves embroiled in battle!

Wine-Based Cocktails

WINE WAS enjoyed in ancient Mesopotamia as long ago as the fourth millennium BC, spreading to Europe by way of Egypt, Greece and Spain. By classical times it was established as part of civilized life. Ancient Greeks and Romans would probably have approved of the use of wine in cocktails, for they considered drinking unmixed wine quite barbaric.

The fall of the Roman Empire also signalled a decline in wine production, which survived chiefly thanks to the Church's use of wine in communion services. Through the Dark Ages the development of good wines and reputable vineyards was due almost entirely to religious houses and pious rulers. By the 12th century, however, wine was back in favour, and production increased. At last, in the 18th century, came a major breakthrough: the introduction of bottles with corks, forgotten since Roman times, enabled vintners to store and mature their product – which until then had been drunk young and raw.

Modern wines fall into four broad categories: still, sparkling, fortified and aromatized. Still wines are the 'natural' form. Sparkling wines can be made simply by pumping in carbon dioxide, the cheapest method, but better versions are achieved by causing a secondary fermentation in a sealed container. Fortified wines, such as port, sherry and madeira, contain added spirit (usually brandy). The techniques were developed in the 1750s, originally to improve keeping qualities on long voyages. Finally, aromatized wines such as vermouth are infused with herbs or other flavours. All have their place in the world of cocktails.

Buck's fizz

This classy cooler takes its name from Buck's Club, London, where it was popular in the 1920s, but is said to have been first invented by the French.

1 measure freshly squeezed orange juice
2 measures champagne

Pour the orange juice into a tall champagne flute and add the champagne, well chilled. There are several popular variations. Substitute peach juice for the orange, and you have a Bellini; or replace the fruit juice with Guinness for a smooth Black Velvet.

LASTING QUALITIES

When vintners began fortifying wines with brandy, they were concerned with improving the product's keeping qualities: the development of port, sherry and madeira as fine drinks in their own right was a bonus. However, in December 1999, archaeologists discovered just how well a fortified wine can keep. A bottle of 17th century madeira unearthed in Spitalfields, London – the oldest ever tasted – was pronounced 'very fresh'.

Champagne Cocktail

Champagne and celebrations go together, so this
is the ideal cocktail for a special occasion.

Glass dry champagne
2 dashes cognac
1 sugar cube
Angostura bitters
Orange slice or wedge and cherry
for garnish

Saturate the sugar cube with Angostura bitters,
pop it into a champagne glass and add chilled
champagne. Top off with the cognac, and
decorate the glass with the orange and cherry.

COBBLERS

By 1805, a popular confection of sherry, sugar,
lemon and ice was termed a cobbler,
presumably because it 'cobbled up' the spirits as
a cobbler restores shoes. Charles Dickens
termed it a 'wonderful invention' in his novel
Martin Chuzzlewit, and its descendant the
Champagne Cobbler merits the same respect.

THE MEN IN THE IRON MASKS

Champagne production took off in the 19th
century, but there were technical problems.
The most dangerous was the exploding bottle.
In hot weather, bottles were so prone to
blowing up during the crucial second
fermentation as gas pressure rose that
cellarmen wore protective iron masks.
Eventually, the day was saved by improved
methods of controlling fermentation and the
development of stronger bottles!

DIJON DELIGHT

Canon Felix Kir (1876–1968), mayor of Dijon,
the 'mustard capital', and one of the heroes of
the French Resistance during the Second
World War, is credited with inventing the
recipe for Kir.

Champagne Cobbler

An old-fashioned favourite, originally made with sherry, is given the modern touch with sparkling champagne and a touch of curaçao.

1 glass champagne
1 teaspoon curaçao
1 teaspoon gomme syrup
Ice
Fruit slices to garnish

Mix champagne, curaçao and gomme syrup; fill a tumbler with ice and pour the mix over ice. Top with slices of summer fruit.

Kir

An old French favourite which was taken up by fashionable restaurants in the 1980s and has lost none of its appeal.

1 teaspoon crème de cassis
Dry white wine

Pour the crème de cassis into a champagne glass and top up with chilled wine. For a Kir Royal, substitute champagne for the still wine. A Kir Lethale includes a dash of vodka and a vodka-soaked raisin dropped into the glass.

Americano

The Italian aperitif Campari provides a deep pink
colour and adds a bitter-sweet tang to
the vermouth.

I measure sweet vermouth
I measure Campari
Ice cubes
Soda water
Slice of orange or twist of lemon peel
to garnish

Half-fill a highball glass with ice cubes; pour in
the vermouth and Campari; top up with soda
water; garnish with orange or lemon.

SHERRY AND VERMOUTH

Dry sherry and dry vermouth go well together.
Try using equal measures of each, with orange
bitters instead of peach, to make a Bamboo, or
with Angostura bitters and a dash of pastis
for a Brazil. For a change, the Adonis uses
sweet vermouth (one measure to two of
dry sherry) with a dash of
Angostura bitters.

WINE AND WORMWOOD

Vermouth is made from white wine, sweetened,
lightly fortified and infused with herbs, notably
the wormwood which gives it its name
(German wermut). The flavour comes from
wormwood flowers, unlike the other famous
wormwood beverage, absinthe, which uses the
leaves. There are many varieties, dry or
sweet, red, white or rosé. French vermouths
tend to be paler and drier than the versions
from Italy.

Greenbriar

The origin of this potion is obscure. It may be named from the Greenbrier district of West Virginia, USA, one of the homes of the Mint Julep.

2 measures dry sherry
1 measure dry vermouth
Dash peach bitters
Sprig of mint to garnish

Stir the ingredients together, and garnish with the mint. This is a refreshing drink, as its vernal name suggests, but also quite potent!

Merry Widow Fizz

Dubonnet, a French vermouth-type aperitif made by adding quinine and other flavours to sweet heavy wine, makes a versatile cocktail ingredient.

3 measures Dubonnet
1 measure fresh lemon juice
1 measure fresh orange juice
Egg white
Soda water

Shake the first four ingredients together, pour into a glass and top up with soda water. For a Dubonnet Fizz, add 1 measure of cherry brandy.

Non-Alcoholic Cocktails

THOSE WHO prefer not to drink alcohol do not have to miss out on the cocktail front: a wide variety of alcohol-free 'mocktails' have been devised for their enjoyment.

Many classic cocktails work just as well without spirits. The best-known example is the Bloody Mary – omit the vodka and you have a delicious Virgin Mary with virtually all the flavour of the original. For a totally tropical cooler, try a Piña Colada without rum, but with an added scoop of vanilla ice cream.

Simple, everyday fruit juices acquire a new dimension when mixed together or given a dash of extra flavouring. Today a wide range of exotic fruit juices is also available, from peach to passionfruit. If you have a blender, you can liquidize your own choice of fruit for a glass full of fresh flavour and vitamins.

All the flavoured cordials, syrups and bitters used in traditional cocktails are available for use in their non-alcoholic cousins. So too are enriching elements like cream, coconut creams and eggs, to say nothing of extras like ice cream and yoghurt. And don't forget, this is your chance to let your imagination run wild when it comes to garnishes!

Pussyfoot

One of the best known 'mocktails', it looks good,
tastes good and even does you good. The
grenadine adds sweetness and vibrant colour.

1 measure orange juice
1 measure lemon juice
1 measure lime juice
Dash grenadine
1 egg yolk
Maraschino cherry to garnish

Shake all ingredients together and strain into a
large cocktail glass or highball glass. Garnish with
a cherry to tone with the rich red colour. This also
makes a refreshing long drink if you top up the
glass with soda water.

TEMPERANCE TIPPLE

The Pussyfoot is named for US temperance
campaigner W.E. 'Pussyfoot' Johnson (1862 – 1945).
As Chief Special Officer of the US Indian
Service, he acquired both his nickname, from
his cat-like tactics when hunting law-breakers,
and his hatred of alcohol, from observing the
misery caused by the 'rot-gut' whiskey trade in
the Indian territories. He became dedicated to
the cause of Prohibition, and gave more than
4000 lectures on temperance.

Yellow Dwarf

Orgeat, a non-alcoholic almond-flavoured syrup,
gives this drink its unusual tang of marzipan and
cheerful colour.

I measure orgeat syrup
I measure cream
I egg yolk
Soda water
Maraschino cherry to garnish

Shake together the syrup, cream and egg yolk.
Strain into the glass, and add soda water to taste.
Garnish with the cherry to set off a drink which is
undeniably yellow, but has nothing
dwarfish about it!

Capucine

The classic after-dinner mint in a liquid form, this
rich and creamy confection is crowned with
grated chocolate or chocolate curls.

I measure peppermint cordial
4 measures fresh cream
Crushed ice
Plain chocolate

Shake the peppermint cordial and cream together;
strain, and add crushed ice. Finally, grate a little
chocolate finely over the top. For a fancier finish,
make chocolate curls: melt the chocolate on a
plate, leave to set, then shave fine curling pieces
off the surface with a sharp knife or peeler.

FRUIT SYRUPS

Home-made fruit syrups make a delicious ingredient for cocktails, alcoholic or otherwise. All you need is ripe soft fruit (raspberries, peaches, etc.) and caster sugar. Mash the washed fruit and leave it in a bowl overnight. Next day, strain off the juice through muslin. Add 8oz/225g of sugar for each halfpint/300ml of juice, and stir over a low heat until the sugar is dissolved. Refrigerated in clean bottles, the syrup will keep for up to a month.

Acapulco Gold

Named for a potent, yellow-leaved form of marijuana from Acapulco, Mexico, this rich, creamy drink is more street-legal than the original but shares the laid-back attitude of the days of 'flower power'.

6 measures pineapple juice
1 measure grapefruit juice
2 measures coconut cream
2 measures fresh cream
1 scoop crushed ice

Shake all the ingredients together. This time, do not strain the result, but pour it straight from the shaker to retain the rich, creamy texture. Decorate with a paper parasol or even a paper flower to set off the delicate colouring.

FANCY FROST

To enhance a sweet cocktail with a sugar-frosted glass, dip the glass rim-first in a saucer of egg white, then into caster sugar. Why stop there? Set off pink or red drinks with a pretty pink frosting by substituting grenadine for the egg white. Instead of sugar, try drinking chocolate powder to please chocoholics, or use 'hundreds and thousands' to decorate a child's glass.

Jersey Lily

This clear, golden refresher is named for the
Edwardian beauty, actress Lillie Langtry
(1852–1929). Whether the most famous of her
lovers, the Prince of Wales (later King Edward VII),
enjoyed it too history does not record.

1 glass fizzy apple juice
Sugar to taste
1 dash Angostura bitters
Ice cubes
Maraschino cherry and apple slice for
garnish

Stir a little sugar into the apple juice, add the
bitters and ice cubes, stir and strain. Spear a thin
slice of apple and a cherry on a cocktail stick to
garnish – or simply drop the cherry into the
bottom of the glass.

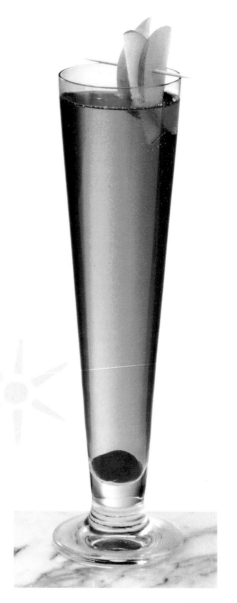

AN APPLE A DAY
Apple juice is a great refresher on a hot day.
For a longer drink, try a Rosy Pippin a glass
of apple juice with a dash of grenadine and a
squeeze of lemon juice, topped up with
ginger ale.

Pom Pom

Lemonade is transformed into an extravaganza that's pretty in pink with a frothy topping to match its frivolous name.

Juice of half a lemon
1 egg white
1 dash grenadine
Crushed ice
Lemonade
Slice of lemon to garnish

Shake the lemon juice, egg white and grenadine together and strain over the crushed ice. Top up with lemonade, and garnish with a lemon slice wedged on to the rim of the glass.

Parson's Particular

You can get more juice out of oranges and lemons if you soak them in hot water for a few minutes before squeezing them. Then let grenadine perform its pastel magic on the juice!

2 measures fresh orange juice
1 measure fresh lemon juice
1 egg yolk
4 dashes grenadine
Cherry to garnish

Shake all the ingredients together, strain into a glass and garnish with a cherry. If you prefer a long drink, omit the lemon juice and top up with soda water for a refreshing Parson's Special.

Useful Tips

CONFUSING RANGE of glasses is available, but there is no need to go out and buy a set of each type. As a general rule, tumblers or highball glasses are suitable for drinks served 'on the rocks', while stemmed glasses are better for cocktails without ice, to help keep them cool. Short cocktails always look good in triangular cocktail glasses, while rounded goblet styles are traditional for drinks which incorporate egg yolks. The larger cocktail goblets have wide rims with plenty of room for flamboyant garnishes. Make sure glasses are sparkling clean by washing them and drying them thoroughly with a glass cloth before use.

Mixed Methods

Cocktails may be shaken, stirred or blended. The aim of all three methods is to combine the ingredients, and at the same time to chill them with ice. It is therefore usually necessary to strain the drink after mixing to prevent too much dilution from the melting ice. Most recipes specify the method to be used, but, if in doubt, as a general rule stir a clear mix, shake a cloudy one and blend a thick one.

Coldness Matters

Cocktails must be cold. Ice serves the dual purpose of chilling and slightly diluting the drink to release the flavours – but the word 'slightly' is important! Chill glasses in the refrigerator before use, or fill them with ice and water and leave them to stand. Bottles of gin or vodka can be popped into the freezer for an hour before mixing to ensure a really cold drink. Ice should be used straight from the freezer before it has time to start melting. Crushed ice is made by wrapping ice cubes in a clean cloth and hitting them with a hammer.

Sticks and Straws

Straws, swizzle sticks and cocktail sticks often form part of the garnish of a drink. Spear your chosen garnish on a cocktail stick and stand the stick in the glass, or rest it across the top of the drink.

Coloured cocktail sticks with sprays of metallic foil as adornment are available for more flamboyant mixtures. Straws can be decorative in their own right, and are available in a range of shapes, colours and lengths. Use fat straws for thick blended drinks.